JAN — — 2018

W9-AAI-374

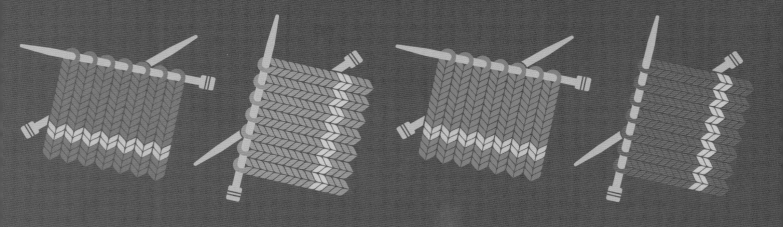

KNITTING

SOPHIE SCOTT

PowerKiDS
press

CONTENTS

GETTING STARTED

Knitting is the art of making loops, called stitches, with a pair of knitting needles and some wool. By moving your needles and the yarn in different ways, you can link all these loops together to make knitted fabric—and then you can create all sorts of things!

This book will show you how to complete several fantastic knitting projects. Each one shows you a new technique to practice and includes a fun twist for you to try once you've mastered the skill. If you ever get stuck, there's a help section at the back.

Don't worry if you feel a bit clumsy holding the needles and yarn at first—it will get a lot easier over time. Focus on following the instructions, and soon you'll be holding the needles very comfortably!

Once you've picked up some essentials from a craft store (see pages 4–5), you'll be ready to start knitting!

EQUIPMENT

You'll be able to find all the following things in any good knitting or craft supply store.

YARN Yarn can be made from wool, cotton, or acrylic fibers—and sometimes it may be a mix. Wool is easiest to work with. Of course, always pick your favorite colors!

Each yarn has a different thickness, and each has a size of needle that matches it. Check the yarn's label to make sure you are buying the correct yarn and needles for your knitting project.

KNITTING NEEDLES

Knitting needles come in different materials, such as bamboo, plastic, and metal. You may find bamboo needles easier at first, since these are not as slippery as metal or plastic needles.

SCISSORS Smaller ones are best for snipping little threads and trimming pom-poms.

TAPESTRY NEEDLE This is a special type of sewing needle with a large hole (called an eye) to fit yarn through, and a blunt tip so the yarn doesn't split.

TAPE MEASURE This is important when checking you are making things the right size.

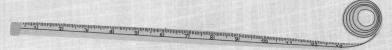

SEWING NEEDLE AND THREAD A sewing needle is thinner and sharper than a tapestry needle. Use it with thread to sew pieces of knitting together.

SEWING PINS AND SAFETY PINS These hold everything in place when sewing your knitting together.

DECORATIVE EXTRAS Felt, buttons, googly eyes, sequins, ribbon … whatever you want to add!

A NOTE ABOUT MEASUREMENTS
Measurements are given in U.S. form with metric in parentheses. The metric conversion is rounded to make it easier to measure.

FABRIC GLUE

CUSHION PAD A bag filled with stuffing that you can use inside a cushion cover.

GLUE Fabric glue is best, but you can always use a blob of white craft glue if you have it.

BASIC BOOKMARK

CASTING ON

This first project covers all the basics of knitting, and you'll have a useful bookmark at the end! Before you start using knitting stitches, you must **cast on** a row of stitches to work from.

YOU WILL NEED

2 ounces (50 g) of double knit (DK) yarn

Scissors

Tapestry needle

Pair of size 6 needles

STEP 1

The first part of casting on is to make a **slip-knot**, which is a special loop that counts as your first stitch. Twist the end of your yarn (called the tail) into a circle, with the tail end lying on top. Fold the tail end in half and pull the folded part through the back of the circle.

STEP 2

Place your slip-knot onto one of your needles and pull the tail so the loop is snug. Hold this needle in your left hand and the other needle in your right hand.

Sometimes the front or back of your knitting work will be mentioned. When you hold your needles, imagine a line along the top splitting them in half. The side facing you is the front, and the side facing away from you is the back.

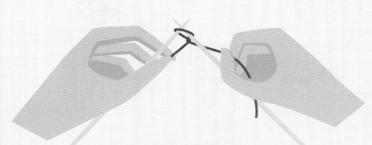

STEP 3

Hold the yarn in your right hand's fingers, behind the needles. Insert the tip of your right hand needle into the slip-knot. Check that the needles make an "X," with the left-hand needle sitting on top.

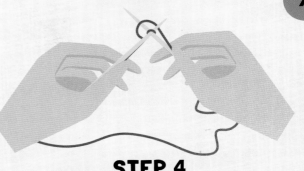

STEP 4

Going from left to right, wrap the yarn around the tip of the right-hand needle, making a little bridge over the top. Make sure you use the yarn coming from the ball, not the tail end!

STEP 5

Slowly slide the right-hand needle back until the tip has come out under the loop on the left needle. You are aiming to catch the little bridge that you just made so it sits as a loop on the right-hand needle.

STEP 6

Insert the tip of your left-hand needle into the new loop so it sits next to the slip-knot.

STEP 7

Now remove the right-hand needle from the loop.

STEP 8

Place your right-hand needle tip in between the two stitches, then repeat steps 4–7. Do this until you have 10 stitches. That will be the width of your bookmark!

KNIT STITCH

Now that you have cast on, you have a foundation to build upon. The next thing you'll need to know to make your bookmark is a knit stitch. The following steps will show you how to do it.

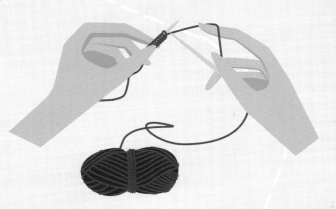

STEP 1

Hold the needle with the stitches in your left hand and the bare needle in your right hand. Hold the yarn with your right hand.

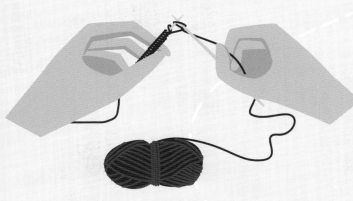

STEP 2

Just as when casting on, place the tip of your right-hand needle into the first stitch, making an "X" with your needles—the left-hand needle should be on top.

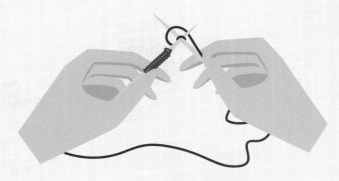

STEP 3

With your right hand, wrap the yarn around the tip of the right-hand needle from left to right, making a bridge over the top of the right-hand needle.

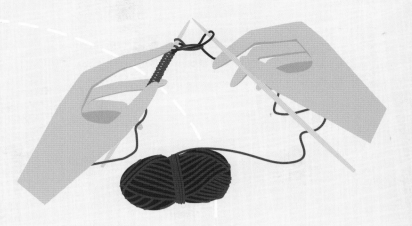

STEP 4

Just as when casting on, slide the right-hand needle back so the tip pokes out from under the loop you entered, then slide it on top of the left-hand needle, bringing the wrapped-around yarn with it.

STEP 5

By sliding right with your right-hand needle, guide the original first stitch up to the end of your left-hand needle and let it drop off. You have now knitted one stitch!

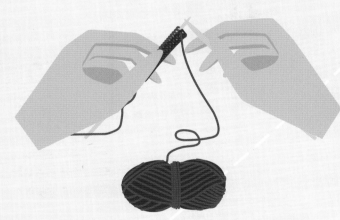

STEP 7

Keep on completing rows of knit stitch until you have a rectangle about 6 inches (15 cm) long.

STEP 6

Continue repeating steps 2–4 until every stitch has moved to the right-hand needle. You have finished a row! Now swap your needles, so you have all the stitches on the left needle and an empty needle in your right hand.

When your work is made up entirely of knit stitches, you have made a knitting pattern called garter stitch.

CASTING OFF

Once your bookmark is long enough, you'll need to fasten off the stitches so they won't undo. This is called **casting off**.

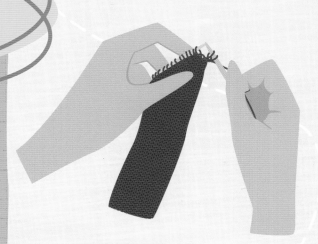

STEP 1
Casting off always requires two stitches on your right-hand needle, so start by knitting two stitches.

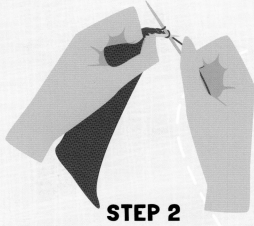

STEP 2
One of these stitches is now going to "leap frog" over the other one and drop off the needle. Do this by picking up the first stitch you just knitted with the tip of your left-hand needle.

STEP 3
As you lift the first stitch over the second stitch and off the right-hand needle, hold onto the tail of the yarn with your right hand to make sure the second stitch doesn't jump off too.

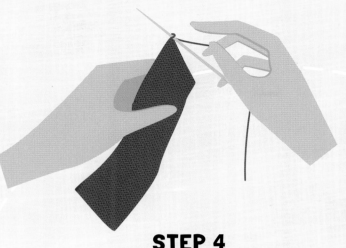

STEP 4

Knit one stitch so you once again have two stitches on the right-hand needle and repeat steps 2–3. Keep doing this until you only have one stitch left on the right-hand needle.

STEP 5

Cut the yarn, leaving a long tail of about 8 inches (20 cm). Loosen the last stitch to make its loop a little bigger, then thread the tail through it, pulling tight.

STEP 6

You will always have tail ends at the start and end of your knitting—and sometimes more if you joined in new yarn. To tidy it, thread a tapestry needle with the tail end and weave the needle in and out of the bumps of knitting on the back side of your fabric. Cut the tail end close to the fabric.

GIFT IT

Bookmarks are perfect for practicing basic knitting skills. Make a few in different colors and hand them out as gifts!

MONSTER FINGER PUPPET

This little monster just wants to have fun! In this project you will use some simple sewing to make the puppet shape rather than casting off as normal.

YOU WILL NEED

2 ounces (50 g) of DK yarn

Scissors

Tape measure

Sewing pins

Fabric glue

Size 6 knitting needles

Tapestry needle

Bits for decoration: googly eyes, felt, stickers, or sequins

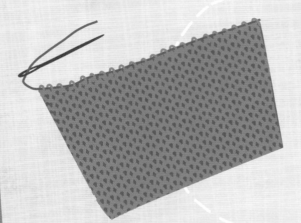

STEP 1

Cast on enough stitches to give you a width of 3 inches (8 cm), then knit until you have a piece that is 2 inches (5 cm) long. Don't cast off. Instead, leaving a length of at least 12 inches (30 cm) for sewing up, cut the tail end of the yarn. Thread a tapestry needle with the long tail.

STEP 2

Using the tip of the tapestry needle, pick up and pass each stitch off the knitting needle and onto the tapestry needle. Keep going until all the stitches are sitting on the tail length of yarn.

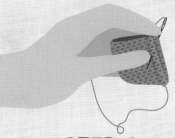

STEP 3

Pull the tail end of the yarn tight. This will make all the stitches gather together and shape the top of the head.

STEP 4

Fold the monster in half and pin the edges. Weave your tapestry needle in between the stitches at the edge of your knitting to sew the puppet together—pass the needle through the fabric, not over it.

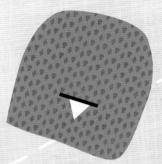

STEP 5

To secure the yarn at the end, keep the last sewing stitch loose. Thread the yarn through this loop and pull tight. **Weave in** any ends and trim any loose tails of yarn.

STEP 6

Now it's time to make your monster come to life! You could try sewing on a mouth, cutting teeth out of felt and attaching them with glue, and adding googly eyes (or just one)!

CLUCK!

Try making animal finger puppets instead of monsters!

COZY COWL

A cowl is similar to a scarf, except the ends are joined together to create a circle. This cowl uses toggles.

YOU WILL NEED

2 × 2 ounce (50 g) balls of chunky yarn

Scissors

Tape measure

Size 15 needles

Tapestry needle

3 toggles

STEP 1

Cast on enough stitches to give you roughly 6 inches (15 cm) of width.

STEP 2

Knit every row. After a while, you will start to run out of yarn from the first ball. Keep an eye on how much you have left—you want to finish the ball at the end of a row, with a leftover strand of at least 4 inches (10 cm).

STEP 3

To start a new ball, lay the leftover strand of your old yarn on top of the tail end of the new ball. Tie the new yarn around the old yarn with a loose knot. Slide the knot close to your needle.

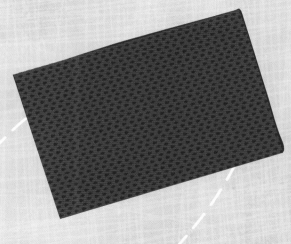

STEP 4

Leave the tail ends dangling and use the new yarn to continue. Keep knitting until the cowl is long enough to wrap around your neck, with a bit extra that overlaps. Once it is long enough, cast off and weave in any loose ends.

STEP 5

Sew the toggles onto the cowl using the same yarn: thread it through the toggles a few times and secure it at the back with a double knot.

STEP 6

Poke the toggles through the other end of the fabric to make your cowl a circle.

KNIT ON

If you would prefer to make a scarf, don't sew the ends together, and keep on knitting! (You'll need a couple of extra balls of yarn.)

STRIPY FINGERLESS GLOVES

Stripes are a great way to include all your favorite colors in only one project. Adding stripes uses the same method as joining in a new ball of yarn.

YOU WILL NEED

2 × 2 ounce (50 g) balls of DK yarn (each one a different color)

Scissors

Size 6 needles

Tape measure

Tapestry needle

Sewing pins

STEP 1

Measure the width of your hand along your knuckles and cast on a width that is double this size in the first color (Color A). Leave a tail end that is 8 inches (20 cm) long for sewing up later. Knit two rows in Color A.

STEP 2

To change color, lay a 4-inch (10 cm) tail of Color A on top of the tail of Color B. Use the Color B tail to tie a knot, so Color A is held inside. Slide the knot close to your needle.

STEP 3

Leave the ends of Color A dangling with the ball of yarn still attached. Now use color B to knit two rows.

STEP 4

Now swap to Color A and repeat steps 2–3. Keep knitting two rows of each color until your piece is large enough to cover your hand from your wrist to your knuckles.

STEP 5

Cast off using either color, leaving a long tail. Cut the tail of the other color too, also leaving a tail.

STEP 6

When you make stripes, the sides of your knitting look different. Fold your knitting in half, so the side you don't want to show is on the outside. Pin this in place, then put your hand on top to measure where the gap for your thumb should be. Use two colored pins to mark the gap.

STEP 7

Thread the tapestry needle with the cast-off tail and sew the sides up to the thumb gap. Then thread your needle with the cast-on tail and sew up the other side of the thumb gap. Remove pins, weave in any loose ends, trim them and turn the hand warmer inside out. Repeat all these steps again to make your second fingerless glove!

EVEN WARMER

Keep knitting to turn your fingerless gloves into arm warmers!

ANIMAL HAT

What's better than a hat?
An animal hat with ears,
a nose, and a mouth!

YOU WILL NEED

2 × 2 ounce (50 g) balls of
brown worsted weight yarn

Tape measure

Sewing
needle and
thread

Tapestry
needle

Size 8
needles

Scissors

2 buttons

Scraps
of felt

Sewing
pins

STEP 1

Measure around your
head and then divide this
measurement in half. This will
be the width of your hat, so cast
on enough stitches to equal that
width. Make sure you leave a
long tail for sewing up later.

STEP 2

Knit enough rows
to make a rectangle
big enough to cover
your head from your
forehead to the back,
plus 4 inches (10 cm)
more, which will be used
for making the ears. When
it is big enough, cast off,
leaving a long tail for sewing
up.

STEP 3

Fold the rectangle in half
lengthways and pin the sides
together. Sew up the two
shorter sides using a tapestry
needle and the cast-on and
cast-off tails. Remove pins,
weave in any loose ends
and flip the hat inside out so
that the **seams** are hidden.

STEP 4

Cut a length of yarn and wrap it round a corner of the hat a few times to make an ear. Knot the yarn several times.

STEP 5

Thread the ends of the ear yarn with a tapestry needle and sew them through to the inside of the hat. Knot the ends again and trim, then repeat steps 4–5 for the second ear.

STEP 6

Cut shapes from felt to make the mouth and nose. Sew them on using a sewing needle and thread. Use buttons for the eyes — knot the end of some thread, then weave the needle through the hat and the holes of the button. To secure the thread, keep your last stitch loose and pass the needle through it, then pull the thread tight.

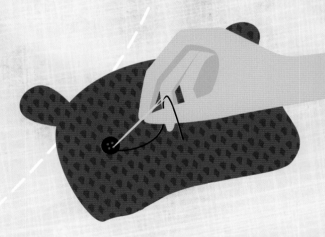

GO WILD

With buttons and some felt, you can make lots of different animals, like bears and squirrels!

POM-POM

What better way to top off your knitting than with a fluffy pom-pom? You'll also need pom-poms to complete the cushion on pages 22–23.

STEP 1

Place the mug on the cardboard and draw around it. Then place the bottle lid in the middle of the circle and draw around that. Cut out the outer and inner circles to create a doughnut shape. Repeat this so you have two.

STEP 2

Wind off a small ball of yarn and wrap the two doughnuts together by going through the hole. Keep going until you can't fit any more yarn through the hole. If you need to add some new yarn, just wind it in.

When the hole gets very small, thread the yarn onto a needle to help you get the last bit through.

YOU WILL NEED

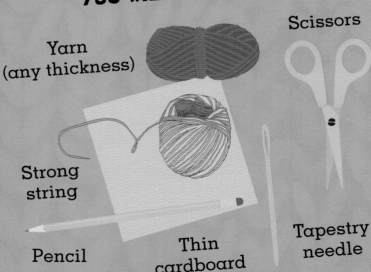

Yarn (any thickness)

Scissors

Strong string

Pencil

Thin cardboard

Tapestry needle

Bottle lid

Mug

STEP 3

Snip the yarn along the outside of the circle, cutting between the two cardboard doughnuts. Make sure you don't pull any strands of yarn loose.

STEP 4

Wrap some strong string around the pom-pom several times, in between the cardboard doughnuts. Tie a few knots to make it secure.

STEP 5

Carefully remove the cardboard doughnuts by snipping the cardboard. Give the pom-pom a little trim with some scissors to tidy the ends. You can cut the string that you used to tie the pom-pom together, or keep it long for attaching to knitting.

GET FUNKY

Try using more than one color in your pom-pom for a multicolor look!

POM-POM CUSHION

This pattern uses knit stitch and a new stitch called purl. Purl is like a back-to-front version of knit stitch. When rows of knit and purl take turns, the pattern is called **stocking stitch**.

YOU WILL NEED

4 pom-poms

Scissors

2 × 2 ounces (50 g) balls of chunky yarn

Tapestry needle

Cushion pad

Size 15 needles

Sewing pins

STEP 1

Measure the width of your cushion pad, then cast on enough stitches to match that width. Knit one row.

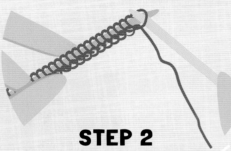

STEP 2

The next row will be purl stitch. Insert the right-hand needle into the first stitch from right to left, sliding it on top of the left-hand needle and making sure that the yarn is at the front of your work.

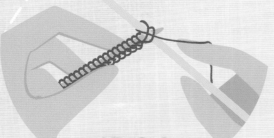

STEP 3

Wrap the yarn counterclockwise around the right-hand needle, so the yarn now lies on the left-hand side of it, at the front of your work.

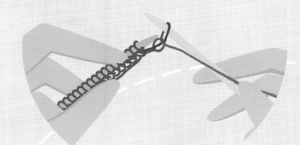

STEP 4

Slide the right-hand needle back until it catches the loop you just wrapped, then slide it under the left-hand needle and use it to slip the original stitch off the left needle. That's one purl stitch!

STEP 5

Repeat steps 2–4 until you have moved all the stitches over to the right-hand needle.

STEP 6

Do one row of knit stitch, then one row of purl stitch. Repeat this until you have enough fabric to wrap around your cushion pad, then cast off.

STEP 7

Fold the rectangle in half with the knit sides touching and pin it. Cut a 12-inch (30 cm) length of yarn and sew down two sides of the cover, leaving one open. Unpin it, then flip the cover inside out. Stuff it with the cushion pad and sew shut with a long length of yarn.

STEP 8

Use the pom-pom tails to sew one to each corner of the cushion. Knot securely at the back of the cushion.

DECORATE

Once you've mastered pom-poms, try experimenting with stripy patterns or button decorations!

PENCIL CASE

Keep your school supplies organized with this knitted pencil case! This project uses a decreasing technique, where two stitches are knitted together, gradually making shorter and shorter rows to create the flap.

STEP 1

Cast on a width of 8 inches (20 cm), then knit enough rows to make a rectangle roughly 6 inches (15 cm) long.

STEP 2

To create the flap of your pencil case, start by inserting the right-hand needle tip into the first two stitches on your left-hand needle.

YOU WILL NEED

Scissors

Size 6 knitting needles

2 ounces (50 g) of DK yarn

1 button

Tapestry needle

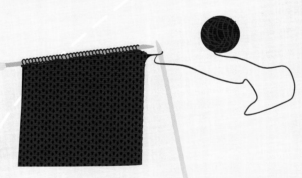

STEP 3

Now continue as if you were making a knit stitch: wrap your yarn around the needle, draw the needle back and catch the new stitch on your right-hand needle. Then guide the old two stitches off the left-hand needle.

STEP 4

Knit across most of the rest of the row, leaving two stitches on your left-hand needle. Knit the last two stitches together as before.

STEP 5

Repeat steps 2–4, knitting two stitches together at the start and end of each row until you have a row that is only two stitches long. Cast off these final stitches.

STEP 6

Sew the cast-off tail back into the tip of the triangle, but don't pull the yarn all the way through—this will be the loop the button will pass through. Sew back and forth in the same spot to secure the loop. Pass the needle through the last stitch, then weave in the ends.

STEP 7

Fold up the rectangle to meet the bottom of the triangle and pin the short sides together. Sew them up with yarn. Remove pins and turn the pencil case inside out.

STEP 8

Place the button on the front of the flap and sew in place with some yarn. Secure it at the back with a double knot.

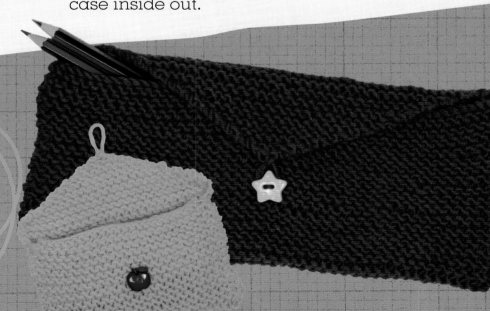

GO MINI

Start off with a smaller rectangle to make a coin purse instead!

BUNTING

Knit a string of flags to decorate your bedroom! In this project you'll learn how to add more stitches to your knitting—this is called increasing.

YOU WILL NEED

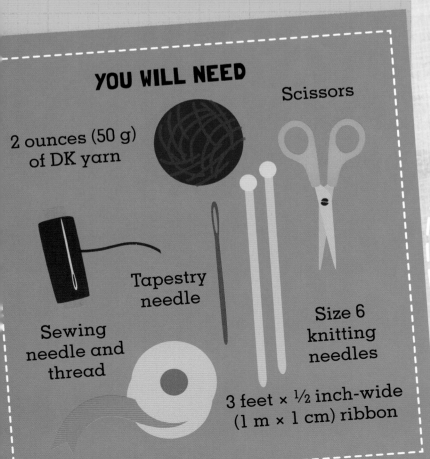

2 ounces (50 g) of DK yarn

Scissors

Sewing needle and thread

Tapestry needle

Size 6 knitting needles

3 feet × ½ inch-wide (1 m × 1 cm) ribbon

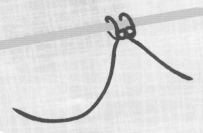

STEP 1

Cast on two stitches, then knit one (tiny!) row.

STEP 2

Increase the first stitch: start to knit as usual but do not slip the stitch off the left-hand needle.

STEP 3

Insert your right-hand needle into the back loop of the original stitch. Wrap the yarn around the needle and knit the stitch. You should have two stitches on the right-hand needle.

STEP 4

Repeat steps 2–3 to increase the second stitch on your needle in the same way. You will have four stitches on your needle. Knit one row.

STEP 5

Now do another increase row: increase the first stitch, knit across most of the row as normal, and increase the last stitch. Knit the rest of the triangle by alternating a knit row with an increase row.

STEP 6

When you have 20 stitches on the needle, cast off.

STEP 7

Repeat steps 1–6 to make five flags. Then weave in their ends and attach them to a length of ribbon using a sewing needle and thread.

POLKA–DOT PARTY

Try using ribbon in a matching color, but with a funky polka–dot pattern, to create a different look.

WHEN KNITTING GOES WRONG

Don't panic if you make a mistake when knitting—there is always a way to fix it. Check your knitting every row or two to make sure everything is on track. As you practice, you'll get used to spotting when something doesn't look right—and you'll have the confidence to fix it!

HOW TO UNDO A KNIT STITCH

STEP 1
For each stitch you need to undo, look for the loop directly under the stitch on the needle. Stretch out your knitting to find the right loop.

STEP 2
Pick up this loop by entering it with your left-hand needle.

STEP 3
Drop the stitch off the right-hand needle. Pull the yarn gently to undo the stitch.

To undo a purl stitch, use the same method, but hold your yarn at the front.

HELP! I KEEP ADDING STITCHES

- Your last stitch from the previous row may have twisted around to look like two stitches, so make sure there is a single loop on the left-hand needle.

- Take care not to split the yarn with your right-hand needle, as this can make multiple stitches.

HELP! I HAVE MYSTERY HOLES

- If you wrap yarn around the needle *before* entering a stitch, you can accidentally make a little hole in your work. Follow the instructions on the left-hand page for undoing stitches.

- Check to make sure you have not dropped a stitch.

- Holes are sometimes made by picking up extra stitches, so check whether your knitting is getting wider.

HELP! MY KNITTING IS REALLY TIGHT

- If you are pulling the yarn very firmly after each stitch, the loops on your needle will be very small. Loosen up and try holding your yarn differently.

- When you wrap a stitch, make sure you are wrapping around the largest part of your needle, not the tip. Wrapping around the thin tip will make smaller stitches.

NEXT STEPS

Now you've learned all the essential steps of knitting, why not try to design your own projects? Graph paper is useful to help you plan your pattern—you can use each square to equal one stitch.

It's always more fun to knit with others. You could start a knitting group with your friends, or even a club at school.

A family member or friend might be able to show you new techniques. Once you have learned knit and purl, there are lots of different ways to combine them to make different patterns.

GLOSSARY

BACK The side of the knitting that will be hidden from view when the project is complete.

CASTING OFF Binding off knitting securely so that the stitches won't unravel.

CASTING ON Creating the foundation row of stitches that will start a piece of knitting.

FRONT The side of your knitting that will be on the outside of your project when you are done. Often this is where the pattern will look best.

GARTER STITCH Fabric that is bumpy on both sides, made by knitting every row.

SEAM A line where two pieces of knitting have been sewn together.

SLIP-KNOT A special loop that becomes the first stitch when casting on.

STOCKING STITCH A type of fabric that is smooth on one side and bumpy on the other, made by alternating rows of knit and purl.

WEAVING IN ENDS Sewing any tail ends of your work back into the knitting so it is neatly finished.

USEFUL WEBSITES

PowerKids Press has developed an online list of websites related to the subject of this book. This site is updated regularly. Please use this link to access the list:

www.powerkidslinks.com/ht/knit

INDEX

Published in 2018 by **The Rosen Publishing Group, Inc.**
29 East 21st Street, New York, NY 10010

Cataloging-in-Publication Data
Names: Scott, Sophie.
Title: Knitting / Sophie Scott.
Description: New York : PowerKids Press, 2018. | Series: Hobby time! | Includes index.
Identifiers: ISBN 9781499434323 (pbk.) | ISBN 9781499434262 (library bound) | ISBN 9781499434149 (6 pack)
Subjects: LCSH: Knitting--Juvenile literature.
Classification: LCC TT820.S36 2018 | DDC 746.43'2--dc23

Editor: Liza Miller
Illustration: Ana Djordjevic, Astound US
Photography: Sophie Scott
Design: Simon Daley

Manufactured in China
CPSIA Compliance Information: Batch #BS17PK: For Further Information contact Rosen Publishing, New York, New York at 1-800-237-9932.